Maps of Small Countries

Also by Russell Erwin
Clear Hills, Empty Sky (Polonius Press)
Taken by the Enemy (Molonglo Press)
From Here (Indigo)
Toward an Imminent Arrival (privately published)

Russell Erwin

Maps of Small Countries

Acknowledgements

The author gladly acknowledges the publications and their editors in which many of these poems were first published: *Axon*, *Quadrant*, *Meanjin*, *The Canberra Times*.

Some of these poems have also appeared in the following anthologies: *Australian Love Poems* (Inkerman & Blunt); *Best Australian Poems 2012, 2014, 2015* (Black Inc.); *The Home Is Not Quiet and the World Is Not Calm*; *Quadrant Book of Poetry*; *The Invisible Thread*.

'And Still' was awarded the Dorothy Porter Poetry Prize 2015.

Another poem selected as part of the Indelible Stencils project (START) has been set up as a 'public poem' in Wee Jasper, NSW.

For my family, especially Isabelle

Maps of Small Countries
ISBN 978 1 76041 158 9
Copyright © text Russell Erwin 2016
Cover image: © Christian Fallini – Fotolia.com

First published 2016 by
GINNINDERRA PRESS
PO Box 3461 Port Adelaide 5015 Australia
www.ginninderrapress.com.au

Contents

Once, In His Boyhood, a Rider Stopped Before Him	7
Crusade for Christ, Villawood, 1960s	9
The Starr family	11
A Memory of Anthracite	14
Off the South Coast	16
A Pew in a House	23
St Andrew's, Moss Vale	25
'*Agape*, from the Greek'	28
On Seeing a Photo of Galilee	30
A Country Swimming Pool	31
Your Names	33
'Hey! Michelangelo!'	34
Two Poems for Isabelle Claire	35
The Kitchen Maid – Vermeer	37
For my parents	39
The Cruel Prayer	48
Weaning, At Any Age	49
Of a Marriage	50
Finding Breath	51
For Two Now Captive of That Moment	53
After your service, Wal	55
A Scene on a Birthday Present's Wrapping Paper…	57
Bloodlines, Stud Breeding	60
Mr Markiel	62
Mr Dunwoody's Voice	63
Around the District	66
Bigga	69
Back Country	70
Meeting the school bus	72
On a Day of Power-line Maintenance	73

Shifting Silage under a Summer Moon	74
Like the Word 'Artesian'	78
The Budawangs	81
In Praise of *Forest Trees of Australia*…	82
As Flames Were My Only Witness	92
Fire at Night	93
Parish Map	95
D Ward	97
The Big Picture	99
The March	101
'…those beautiful young men'	102
Looking for your mob	103
The Coupling of Names and Places, 1941–	104
Ah! The stars of Rajasthan	106
Amritsar	108
The Kathak Dancer: Mandawa, Holi, 2002	109
Lights Across Autumn Paddocks	111
Otters at Mogo Zoo	114
Country Show Fantasy	115
The Autumn Break	116
The Red Enamel Bangle	117
And Still	118
Thinking of Student Accommodation, Glebe	119

Once, In His Boyhood, a Rider Stopped Before Him

A boy is looking up at a rider, high there, under the sun.
Dark wings of shadow spread over him a sudden cold.
He squints as the eclipsed sun flares around her.
He cannot make out her face but is heady
with the clover fullness of the animal.
Stretched, leather gives and creaks.

Suddenly the bay shudders: from the neck,
that crest which in its stressed arch cows a subject people;
all along that length, sleek as a submarine, a rippling
– like satin being smoothed – as if a surplus of electricity
were being discharged through its sexual skin.

One hindquarter rises higher than the other,
is hunched; the hide, the oiled hair of a gigolo, breathes gloss.
It waits. All of it lolling with the attitude of a bored teenager.
And on such finely carved Chippendale legs!
Never has he been as close to something this potent
– that casually, insolently, flexes.

And she restrains all of it! Does nothing but gives and resettles
with each of its props and self-indulgent skitters.
Foam flecks the bit, slobbers like spawn;
salt-sweat gathers between the legs, soaping the girth.
Swollen worm-thick, the craze of veins thrill with its gift.
All over a constant shivering like the nervousness of little birds.

Each nostril dilates pink and exotic and cavernous,
How soft the grey velvet of its sheath.
All of this: immense and delicate.
And it is here, before him:
impatient and wilful and held.

A squeeze: haunched muscle relaxes, distance releases under him,
each hoof cutting neat cups into a summer's fired earth,
each the sharp print of a fine new-moon, even the indent
where the nails go. And the flung clods, the disturbed ground.
And they are gone.

They were here.
He must tell himself this.
He touched that skin.
Its sweat dries on his fingers.
Like a lover knowing what is being lost he looks,
keeps looking down that street, until lost,
they enter his past: that easy gait, that girl balanced,
rocking, disappearing, scented and improbable
and beckoning.

In the hollow of that afternoon he is cold.
At his feet, hoofprints and the white roots
of the upturned clods clutching.

Crusade for Christ, Villawood, 1960s

A maggot bloated there on the vacant corner block.
A half-emergent airship, entered via an airlock
to crushed grass, stale air, body odour,
and voices distorting in the pressure,

like a ringing in your ears
after an afternoon at the pool.
When they got serious though,
the God bit, you had to get out.

Salvation, being reborn, committing your life –
this was scary stuff and that word, 'death',
like the stink of damp seeping
through an old couple's house.

And those chook-eyed women
(was Heaven as joyful as they?),
too young to know of sex
still I knew they were bloodless.

When they spoke it was like cloth flapping.
And something about the Team Leader,
his lovely voice, his eyes doey,
because this was how Christ must have been
and this was the face of love.

Out! Back to a weed-tatty paddock,
litter like scuts of dirty snow,
and the glitter of broken glass. But
here was landfall, the familiar earth!
The scour of eucalyptus.

Yet in that moment, as if squirming
from a vice of fingernails, the unusual gift
and weight of freedom. Which way to turn?
You knew you were spurning Eternal Life.

And even a parent's love – her wings,
his mountain, could not protect
from the cold of knowing this.

I felt wetness between my toes,
a bright smile of glass had cut my foot.
There freely, my blood! The warmth
of it as it bled,

while behind me the pulse of happy-clappy music
and every now and then, clearly, the words,
'He brings me joy, joy, joy
into my heart. He brings me joy.'

The Starr family

She'd pass our front gate as she walked up the long hill from
    the town
to school. I contrived to join her until it was clear she didn't
    need
my company. Nothing said, just politeness, her head held
the way a dressage horse is, under rein. And then, those eyes
noting something insufficient retired, like a woman
who, declining a caller, returns down a hallway and disappears.

She walked as good-looking girls do – assured, self-contained,
her long, thick, black, black hair, plaited and hanging,
straight as rectitude, swinging slightly like a counterweight.
    Her hips.
In class she barely spoke, keeping to one or two other girls.
Yet there was something slyly innocent, sensual, mocking,
in the way she would look at the idiocies of boys who didn't
    realise
what a doe-eyed Jessica was among them.

Once, with my mother on the train back from Sydney
I shared a dog-box with her family. As soon as we'd settled
into a compartment, thickly foreign with the headiness of
    real coffee,
her mother offered bagels and lox, which mine accepted,
    somewhat primly.
The daughter read and so escaped, while I sweltered
all the lurching way home in a sauna of fantasy and
    competing perfumes.

That act seemed such an unusual generosity.
Not a bridge or prelude to anything, just generosity.
And gracious too. Yes, a graciousness, a refinement,
that was not assumed or mannered. Yet my mother
would sometimes say, 'It's not hard to see why.
They set themselves apart.'

Once, my parents returned from a slide evening at church
of a trip Mrs Starr and her husband had made back to Europe.
Mum woke me and couldn't stop telling me – then, and the next morning.
Especially of walls pocked, scutched, cross-hatched
by innumerable tiny claws.
'Why would this be so?' Mrs Starr had asked.
The hall silent. All eyes glazed by one of the slides
– the smoothness of tiles. So clean. White as innocence.

In the same way a sufferer wears a shadow
by which their condition sets them apart
they lived in that country town with what they were:
witnesses – that history was not terrible or remote.
It was terrible but it was warm and near,
as surely as the breath is; it was words
ever in their heads, as real as bread or prayer,
present like a briar, while another generation,
under this, other sky, unfolded leisurely about them.

Once a mate taunted as Mr Starr drove past
on his newspaper round, 'Go on. Dare you.'
I did. Of course.
'Hey, Jew', '… You dirty Jew',
'…fucken Jew'.

I thought I'd gotten away with it
but thirty yards later the car stopped.
A kind of weariness emerged –
as if an ageing boxer once again
were returning to the ring.
A sadness shaking the bulk of him,
'Do you know what you have said?
And your father, he is a good man.'
I knew.

Currawongs let loose their last marbling calls,
each house hunched like cattle as night thickened.
I stood there in the early chill.
Out of my mouth – those words.

A Memory of Anthracite

In bed I felt the moisture of my breath
mist the cold rock, and could not sleep.
In the dark a day was forming which had walls,
impervious as death and as black,
and as terrifying, as the face of God.
With the first step of descent I knew
the safe, daily earth would open up
like treachery and reveal how the dark
is just beneath our feet, where light
is as precious as air, and how easily
it might be taken from us and there'd be
no return. I could not sleep.
And the word they'd told me – 'anthracite'
had the clinical menace of a silent planet
silted through its cold letters. It shone
in my head like water off hard planes of rock.

Then out of a bushland dripping with mist
in the school-grey dawn the stricken angularity
of rust-sad machinery, and as if pasted onto the side
of the mountain, like in the cartoons, a black, elliptical 'O'.
Standing at the shaft's mouth, light bitten clean as an apple,
I knew the hollow self.
Even the timber props were puny, cracks in them opening
into their own darkness, and from hairline fractures
water seeping in like quiet workers.
A different air swelled from beneath,
gutted of the spices of the flowering earth,
full of the dark and overpowering the breath
with all the bluster of an ancient god.

Only one hundred yards in, I turned,
and back there, that gaping 'O'. Daylight
diminishing now like a previous life. Further in,
some men watched we visitors, were amused
or noting the lamp-white of fear, turned their backs
and resumed working. They could have been there forever,
coming in and out of the shadows, as if darkness
were clothes they lived in easily.

Later, released back to the smell of eucalypt,
the larruping of currawongs, I saw one of them
as he emerged from the shaft and from his glance
felt the thoroughness of his contempt –
as if everything above ground, even daylight
was anaemic, somehow effete, whereas his days
caged among timbers adjusting to a shifting mountain,
damp with the infiltration of water,
tuned to the uncertainty of rock, were worn
in a light which at any moment might leave him.
His days spent face to face before those shining walls,
his body ingrained with its black
and in his eyes what he knew,
which we in our light-filled lives
would not, could never.

Off the South Coast

As a small boy the night before I could not sleep: was
   bobbing and adrift.
Then, first light was galvanised iron. And spread before us,
   lazing,
rucked like a sheet this other I had known only as a word: the
   ocean.
Our tinny, thin-skinned, skittish as a colt, wavelets lapping
   the side,
the slap, slap as easy and familiar as an uncle. Lace doilies of
   foam opening
across the greasy dishwater-green and oil film of the shallows.

It is all bustle, joking among men, the big bones of their
   laughter,
the serrated edge of banter, the bilious fume of bait and fuel,
   the clumsiness of gear –
all this, accumulated, necessary for the passage from one
   element to another –
and we, not unlike the masts of passengers among their bags
   at an airport.

The engine coughs, gurgles as if being drowned, then
   challenges the clammy air
with an exuberance of its plashing, its deep-throated self-
   confidence
and easily the grey town looks like rind, like proud flesh, and
   recedes.
So too, the backdrop mountains – they slide down the sky,
   become a line, are erased.

Now is talk-time, getting settled, laughter, 'Hey! Watch
   where you put that.
Could do y'self a damage!' 'Doan worry, mate. Damage's been
   done!'
and then stillness as each looks out, around, back.
And it is fresh. No other word intrudes.

Spray needles our skins, the thump, thump, slap. Blue water.
   Blue sky. And thump.
Then the longer, deeper, heavier thump, wait and drop. And
   thump again. The tinny cracks,
but the engine knows no master and we are headed out of
   our depth. The men
are happy. They are away from their inland town; they are
   together as men-as-boys,

as they were in the war. They are teaching their boys, they are
   broaching like bottles
of D.A. what inland, inside, keeps capped, and they are
   bragging. They are out of their depth
and happy. White caps froth like the head on a schooner.
The swell rises and falls like a sleeping man's belly. All day we
   allow the sun to roll
over us its masseur's hand. All day – lines glint as if cut in
   glass; small Escher worlds
bead and run. At the point of disappearance a nick like the
   incision from keyhole surgery.
To this is given the devotion, the not-quite casual hope
   usually given to lotto numbers.

Then zing! Like a fence wire singing, a jettisoning of pearls
    from an unstrung necklace, and there, the way
a face resolves in a dream, a shape ascends and breaks the
    surface.
Like hauled treasure – red ugliness and streamlined, glittering
    beauty now threshing.
For minutes in the slosh suffering flaps then weakens, hardens
    to a glaze
at the bottom of the boat, that is only a skin's thickness deep.
    And the businesslike water slaps.

The day wheels into another quarter of the sky. And there is
    no direction here.
Where's home? The sun takes itself away like someone
    slipping into a café.
Where's home? The glittering water drops its glitter. Is dull
    like the fish
at the bottom of the boat, is matter-of-fact. Curt, dismissive.
    Cool.

It won't start. There is the pretence: a sputter, a whine of the
    starter
until like a complaining child, exhausted it trails away: a puff
    of exhaust, a kick,
a shudder. But not together. The engine is sullen, sculptural,
    an object from a museum.
And still.

We hadn't realised but about us the simplicity of a great
    world: sky, water, the erratic wind, daylight.
No other: not the scurf of shops, a thread of highway lights,
or even the jumbled constructions of mountains, the green
    population of trees.
This world is huge and solid like walls. I think of Antarctica
    towering over Shackleton.

This has no ego: it just is and works. Milling, shuffling,
    jostling, thumping the hull,
all things like dough between hands. And we are losing
    daylight.
It is withdrawing from us. We, like creatures of curfew,
    withdraw too.

As if attending to a shrine, the men offer themselves to the
    intestinal, Byzantine anatomy
of a machine in which we've placed our faith: to the intrigues
    of oxygen, fuel, spark,
to our confidence in metal; doubts now surfacing, knowing
    the treachery of oil and water.
We have no solid ground. Our earth is only a skin's thickness.
    And we are out of our depth.

The owner, simple as a machine, confident in his machine,
   hums and puffs, swears mildly,
'She'll be right. It sometimes does this. Did I tell how it broke
   down when we was…'
All our stuff is strangely foreign to us now. We are open now
   as if on a vast stage
and have no need of anything but the certain breath . Our
   voices call out like actors.

It's dark. Hollowed, we hunch. The air cling-wraps us in its
   cold.
We withdraw into a refuge of words we will not say, as if
   talismans, as if anchorage,
and talk to ourselves as though setting-off down different
   roads,
clutching prayers, hopes, silly humour. And we drift.

Not as we do, through the fog of our days with its names,
its clamouring voices but for the first time, stripped.

Water is black, the sky floured with scintillant stars. Jets trail
   their blinking markers.
The men resume what they were: the quiet one, the joker, the
   one last invited, the doer.
And their sons see them as they are, here undisguised on this
   bent sheet of metal.
A boy begins to whimper, his father cuffs him. 'Don't be a girl.'
The blood from this cut will colour us like the memory of a
   staining sunset.

We sit and learn to accept the whale's hump of the swell lift,
   then the dump,
only to rise and rise and sicken until we fall, again. There is
   only menace,
of things moving easily below you, things in their natural,
   unforgiving element,
and the seductive distraction of pattern – moonlight, broken
   and scattered,
rippling and shifting and disorienting like a work of Op Art.

Stiff, we swap positions, stretch, look. And keep looking
   because we ache
for what the unvarying sea will not give. There is the option
   of sleep.
'Put your head down, son.' Sleep is as necessary as luxury.
   Some do or try.
The facts are sky, water, and our craft. The elsewhere, never-
   ever of home.
The smell of my father. The smallness of me.

The night is veined like onyx. By looking into any of its depths
you could disappear. Everything out here is simple. I know I
   am weak.
I look at my father. And know I can know nothing more
   about him,
other than that he too is a vessel, though his strength will
   outlive me
the way some civilisations in their ruins are more vital than
   our own.

Somewhere, Ha! Somewhere, maybe out of sleep, out of the dark,
the engine kicks into life. 'I knew it,' the owner says. 'Always,
 the fuel lines.
I'll take a look at it when we get back. Always knew. She'll be
 apples.'

No. It's not into life. The result of supplication? Maybe.
Holding the mouth right? But the motor only fires into its
 sequence.
No. We who drifted have been woken. Now, the bluff man is
 quiet,
as he looks at the shy one, who looks back steadily as he does
when he looks up at his allotment of sky, accepting it.

This the son notices, which he'll keep like a love letter.
The worker, the one given to giving, looks at his hands.
His son, who doesn't understand, still doesn't but will not
 fight it.
And will, one day, learn his way into love.

Early light reshapes the boat, gives to faces a softness of grey
 chamois;
as our eyes, the eyes of an immigrant, look for, then lose,
 then are given
a hard seam, like coal – a coast, a new land. For this is not
 what we knew
when we left. There is still the scumble of a town, makeshift
 as a film set,

but when we step ashore it is not onto solid ground
and for nights after, for a long time, waves slap along a hull,
testing the skin.

A Pew in a House

Gaunt and severe as the gaze of any elder,
From a kirk like the one I knew
This pew now in a suburban house
Is jetsam and relic.

Aloof, it forbids use,
An unbending Presbyterian.
Captive, bearing mute witness
To a frivolous, ungodly people.

Its wood rubbed by work –
Devotion, faith, supplication, doubt.
Too hard for ease
This seat had to be endured.

Its first lesson: still the body.
This hardness then was harness
For a collar-proud soul: but then
It ached: all those wasted hours.

Words hammering down, over, upon us,
Pleading, exhorting, bullying a congregation
While light fired the memorial window
And broke in spattered pattern across the aisle.

All those hymns, sermons, prayers.
And I remember hands clasping the edge
Of the pews – mostly dairy-farmer's,
Fingers thick as teats,

Misshapen from the ever-bawling hunger
Of cows and calves,
So used to weight their hands were useless
Here in the weightlessness of prayer.

Thick with the smell of their cows
And Old Spice I remember backs
Hunched like boulders,
The cloth of their jackets straining,

Some breathing hard, as if from work,
The Word working in their mouths like cud,
As they buckled to the hard task of silence.

St Andrew's, Moss Vale

In that little church with paddocks dreaming to the west,
I learned the infinite space of prayer. It expanding
until words hurt and fizzled out, confused and incoherent.
How I floundered, same as when
the shallow end of the swimming pool gave way
and nothing was beneath my feet. No one knew
you were drowning, all you wanted was the surety of air.

But there was peace too – a congregation breathing deeply
like the slow lift and settle of the sea. A music in words,
and their muscle too: they worked, were worked
and became the Word that breathed. 'Mary kept all these things
and pondered them in her heart.'

On any morning a splay of light over the blue and gold
fleur-de-lys runner was like air scented by a lemon flowering,
and sometimes was a yellow square, warm with the hope
that God might live not in the chill corners, the forest of words,
the hammered wood of the hymns but outside, in life, in the sun.

A cotoneaster outside scraped the frosted glass,
its shadows scoring like whip marks on the floor.
When prayer defeated me I'd stare at the broad cypress boards,
each knot and whorl, spiralled, like constellations,
and wound tighter and tighter into a black

that seemed to be at the centre of everything.
God was there somewhere but beyond any words I knew.
Knowing this, I knew I was alone.
And this would not change.

This place, that hour: the clamminess, on faded blue hymn
  books
mould grew into capes and bays around which my bored
  fingers traced,
the pinched stink of mice-urine, shadows heavy as wool-black
  curtains,
the sweep of the cypress trees outside at the time of the
  Benediction.
Sweep. Sweep. Sweep.

And how quickly, out in the vestry with the counting of the
  collection
language, relaxed, changed its clothes. The loosening of ties
gave it away. How like an espaliered tree springing back being
  set free.

As they counted the money for the missions, the stipend,
the image I could not dispel:
'From his hands, his head, his side, his feet',
That face, haunting as a junkie, staring. Wanting.

And burning for us all, this church of the burning bush,
our white-haired, crew-cut Scots minister
who with a fist clenched and swinging, leaned far out from
  the pulpit
as if to demonstrate how faith could ignore gravity, chastised
  each

our fecklessness and infidelity, our poverty, and grieved,
'Oh! Brrotherrs and sistors in Chrrist, I implore ye,
Turrn ye again. Turrn.'

Chafing, yet no one stirred.
Crickets scritched outside, other insects whirred,
hazing the light out on the porch
repeatedly blundering.

'*Agape*, from the Greek'

A crucifixion each Scripture lesson he gamely fronted,
the all-too decent pastor who even the good kids
took part in goading. Teachers waited in the corridor,
delighted to storm in and restore order.
All of us smirking.

He, filled with the love of the Word,
how through tongues and translations,
thrilled the clear living water of God's love.
He, nervous with the terribleness, the terror of it,
of how faith was a sheet blowing,
where there was no anchor.
And the self, what was that?

How there was no other to aid him:
who else could know the bleak moors of text,
the blank rock face?
Or that sometimes, a sudden upland of light,
an alpine daisy, its lifted head.

Here waking each day in a parish of dairy farmers,
the knives of small meannesses, their contempt
for the wateriness it was agreed was the most
he could give, and their resistance to join him
enduring the desert, the bereaving waters, the cold
light years within a text, seeking the washed face
of salvation, the diamond light.

I am grateful to him though for opening
that one word in the infinitely unfolding poem
which is the first chapter of John:
'…and the darkness comprehendeth it not.'

And for his frail, honest courage, respect.
And this prayer: in the light blue
of his eyes a shard of ice might harden,
might stare his God to account:

'Why? What did you want from me?'

On Seeing a Photo of Galilee

Its name, a bubble, a gabble
like any sound repeated over,
at best a noun in a valley of stories,
those stones come tumbling to us,
which as they fall make our rough map.

So it was a surprise to see in a photo
of the skies over Galilee, a hill
– napped close-rugged in green felt
like a shearer's handpiece – and

an orchard. Not what I imagined –
all desert, arid as text,
its blinding sands, its white bones of dispute
but the sense here there would be

the suddenness of blossom,
there would be fruit, the singing of the pickers,
and then above, the blue and torn clouds
– it had to be spring!

And that this was the sky
that Christ had looked up into,
smelt the bursting air
and wondered.

A Country Swimming Pool

(for Alexandra & Hugh)

This substitute for beach, for the blue,
incomprehensible blue-other place of ocean,
-its infinity, its ozone, its insolent competition,
bodies stripped to their confidence,
and the defeat of the shy,
this inland water is an island:
three mothers, their toddlers,
kids on summer holidays skylarking
and me.

My children run, giddy from turquoise water,
which spills in large pearls as each shakes
the shaggy, loose drapery of it off,
runnels worming down their backs,
– the Channel country shining silver in flood;
cold-shivery pimpling their skins, their white skins;

their hair, rust-streaked, ropey, sticky, finger-combed,
or lacquered flat – with that louche sickliness affected
by models. Their heads sculpted back to bone,
bare and fraught as when they were the infants I'd held;

and maps of small countries drying at their feet,
like those they slip into as they shelve into sleep.
Chlorine clings like a crust; they smell like a laundry floor.
Through chattery teeth,
'Come in, Dad. Come in,'
then immediately dive back
like darters ducking under the surface of the dam,
breaking splash all over in a spray of cool glitter.

They are animal with water, with being in water,
with water being as easy as air, with their bodies just being:
they're yet to know what currency it is other than this – delight.

I stand at the edge, and look as they surface,
feeling foolish and pleased, and somehow lost, and old,
as light dazzles little stars from the crinkled water their heads
   poke through,
their water-puckered, old persons' faces as dreamily
they look up at me:
'It's beautiful in, Dad. It really is.'
This sapphire lagoon fringed by squeals and splashes,
– its water smashed and scattered and smashed again
by their giggling, unsuspecting bodies.

Your Names

I hear your names,
the ones I gave you,
used by people
whom I don't know.

In the mouths of strangers
they're marbles or coin,
not what I heard when I toyed
their syllables while
you were as yet unborn.

And I want to keep them
just as I want to keep you
– as syllables in the blood,
in my heart and unspoken.

'Hey! Michelangelo!'

(Postcard from my daughter and son-in-law on their honeymoon)

Bluest of heaven, heavenly blue,
impossibly blue, softest, downy blue,
blue vein of a milking breast-blue,
that soused and lazy sea of all our dreams,
background out of which comes creation,
His Creation. Ours. This
the plaster-cream, the sullen grey,
the tinctures of rose and pink,
the rotundity and plasticity of flesh,
its slackness and sinews too.
All crowding and milling,
tumbling and fecund with busyness,
all grieving their mortality,
teeming and blind like new-born mice in a box,
glutinous as boiled rice.

I rather like the obverse,
    'Hey! We're in Vatican City
    Its lovely – Just seen Sistine Chapel – WOW!
    Rome is fabulous,
    Love to all.'

Hey, it doesn't get any better than that
does it, eh, Michelangelo?

Two Poems for Isabelle Claire

Peaches, Somersby

I felt firmness touching your mother's, my daughter's, belly
and finally the poem is finding its way to utterance
which has been with me even before she was born,
coming to me when we stayed on a magical orchard
where the family there were bright and blushed as their fruit
and I met their firstborn in among gusts of mist
and cups of tea and great projects undertaken gladly
and that day walked out among the ripening peaches
immediately after a shower of rain,
wisps of mist clinging to branches weighed heavy and dripping,
and saw the shy curve of fruit firming into fullness,
their bloom the texture of the newborn, soft and radiant,
and the scent, the scent. The earth and its heaven-scent.

The Gift

We took our baby to meet her.
My senile grandmother, lumped
in a corridor of that home, reached
like a bare twig, at this thing
that seemed quite beyond her,
the cocoon which was your mother,
stroking, smiling, not really knowing
what it was she held. And your mother,
so profoundly asleep, as you are now,
never knowing that moment either.

In that half-hour, among the factory noise
of that place, that woman, who in part, passed
on this equivocal gift, and your mother, met
and touched.

Down the corridor there was an eruption of voices
as we stood in that silent room,
like the Magi, lost at the margin of wonder,
and grieving too.

The Kitchen Maid – Vermeer

(for Margaret)

The house murmurs, stirs – the mistress
in the front parlour, who has instructed her to this,
the butcher's boy at the back gate about to knock,
even sparrows flitting onto flagstones from the elm,
the toss and curtsy of leaves in a courtyard breeze.

There are these lives – the light is scented with them,
in the same way it is pale and yellow with the scent
of a lemon tree beyond the scullery window.
It breathes the bread with yeast-fullness
and fills the crust, the house with calm and order.

But what you see is a girl in a linen cap pouring milk.
Solid, conscientious, taking care not to spill,
for here even the light does not do that.
Steadily milk froths in the jug,
white and blue as it fills.

Yet she is unaware how she is touched:
along her left forearm as if dusted in flour,
the broad sweep across her forehead,
how her collar whitens, being laundered;
how intimately it favours the back of her right hand.

This light, like any casual gesture of love, surprises
with its flooding gift and delights her skin.
Her blood responds. On her cheek a blush
like the down of an apricot ripening.
As freely as is given to her it is given to us:
we breathe the same still air,
hear the milk gurgle as it pours,
damp rises from the corners,
the cold pooling at our feet.

Our faces too are lit by what completes her –
this light on a painted surface,
sure from the painter's hand, sober and clear,
is immanent with grace, rare with grace.

Although in the quiet, somewhere, we hear,
unhurried, the working of a clock.
Each second comes, lives a life,
and in the chill, is lost.

For my parents

A Present from Christmas Last

I toss the shirt into the wash –
to rid it of its factory must.
A gift from my father,
though he didn't choose it.

My sister did – shopping
being for him out of the question
Christmas last.

This gift seemed more a duty
being fulfilled. When I thank him
he looks at me blankly.
He has no idea.

Among all the gifts he gave
this the last
and he has no idea
why I kiss him, and kiss him again.

In this, the third week after his death
I toss a new shirt into the wash.
And watch it tumble then submerge
along with everything else.

Too Late

Two streets up the hill from here
my father is asleep, I hope.
But I know he is not.
He waits for daylight,
to be up and doing.
My mother, his wife, his only girl,
he has nursed and has buried.

It's late, too late.
I do not want to disturb him
and slip through town,
hoping that with distance
and the soothing moonlight
a reason not to call might seem right
and I'd not have to face
what he tries to hide.

Oh! My father! Caretaker
of a house that is just a house,
cold in the moonlight. No.
Not now, not tonight.

His Text

He still gets up before me, his criticism of me
as a farmer is I'm not up early enough,
seeks out work as seed hungers for the light.

Most mornings he stands before me –
with a cup of tea, 'Rise and shine.'
It gives me the shits.

He stands there
– his face unsullied by the world,
– pink, clean as scrubbed pork.

He has beaten cancer, legionnaires' disease,
the punishment he took on at work,
though he's never spoken about himself –

what little I know comes from others.
Even Mum didn't know much.
Gives himself but not to himself

as if there is no self. No point
in family history, only family, only us.
Cannot sit and chat.

There are dishes to be done.
Knows nothing about cars, machines.
Has never spoken of women. His vice: church.

Intemperate, simple prejudices, simple politics.
Wary of flashness, spivvy types, of bull.
His humour – belly laughter, not wit.

Genial, warm, but you'd never forget the Calvin cold
in the blue ice of his dismissal. Utterly unforgiving
of moral flaw. The mark of an innocent man.

Travels miles to come here to the farm,
'Be there by six. You be up, hear.'
When work's finished he'll abruptly leave

and even in his eighties, drives back,
a danger to traffic but implacable,
because there're things he has to get to.

It was a sign the time he agreed to stay.
But now he is here before me.
He has lost his girl.

The only one he ever had.
He doesn't speak, he weeps.

After the March, Lewisham '05

He has recovered from his wife's death
as much as ever he will, though it's clear
all's in place, ready to act in his dying
that's two years away from this month.
But today he's in his best suit, bright, still the head
of his family as we walk across the park
where as a boy he saw O'Reilly and Bradman play.
Then I see him drift behind and without a word,
turn back down the path, firmly, surely,
the way I'd always seen him leave the house for work.
His pace quickens till it's almost a jog trot, a scurry
but it's no use.
He reappears from the toilet block,
this shy, self-contained, self-abnegating man,
soiled underpants in hand, stands dazed and shrunken.
A jogger clips him and he collapses.
He finds his feet and straightens.
'You right, Dad?'
For the briefest second those blue eyes weaken
and search me for an answer I cannot give
then look back steadily, bleakly, fiercely,
'Fine, fine. I'm fine. You go on. *Go on.*'

Returning for a Minor Operation

(for my brother, Greg)

I haven't been to the Holy Land but expect I would feel that way:
the sense that at the site of the Garden or the wall of the old city,
among the continual passage of feet, of breathing, gabbling people
I was stepping on ground where He had stepped on his way to me.

I had it in Old Delhi: the dust in the streets, the Murghal bricks:
everywhere we breathe in yesterdays and tomorrows,
so many of them, turning over, ploughing under, returning
in a street-seller's bad-teethed smile, the kites winging over.

What I can't accept but have to sidestep, blur over,
is that I am in the same place today as where we'd left you,
the ward where you stumbled in your hazed comprehension,
with the last of your bullock strength made a hobbled rush

for an exit, like a beast in the slaughter yard,
while we steered you, you who'd held us,
we, who'd followed in your footsteps around the garden,
led you back to a bed and a couple more months.

4th August 1952

I have a photograph of you on your wedding day,
St Lucia Methodist Church, 4th August 1952

but I want to hear what the wind heard
– for I gather it was a blustery day –

as you step from the car your veil becomes flighty –
and want to know what the light witnessed,

what it, and only it, could witness
between you two as the car pulls up

and faces fill the window, their greeting, their desire
to share the magic of a bride, confirming this is your day.

Your father, the clean lines of his intelligence,
the bright, observant eyes, what did he say

to you, his veiled daughter, his shy shadow,
clouded in vulnerability, you, my slight, innocent mother?

What silly rot, what bit of nonsense, to ease your trembling,
knowing what it is you'd step out into: the unknown

of a marriage you thought you might not ever have,
though to a man who would love you in the only way

that matters, and were, I'd say, happy. What did he say?
What could any father say as the wind lifted your veil?

Flowers on the Sideboard

(i.m. my mother)

Though most stand in their vases,
stiff, resisting the inevitable,
today from the bunch of flowers
the church sent back
some petals fell.

From silence to silence
they fell, softly down, floating
as do little boats of marigolds
setting out on the Ganges.

I heard them brush the sideboard.
One more detail, like the clock ticking
more loudly than usual, or the slant
of dust-motes through the blinds,

that's widening the gap from the day
they decorated the church for you
– one more thing moving you away.

For Colleen

Cleaning up, years after, I find –
'for Colleen' – For who?'
Then I remember – the twisted mouth,
the cables and wires of a constricted neck,
making her look like an alarmed turkey,
all her left side like a drawn bow aiming skywards,
a blotched, roughened skin you wouldn't want to touch.
She, the one with a mop. She,
among all the staff in the Stroke Ward,
who crabbed her way over to my mother and sat
and stroked her hair
and talked with her
as though they were equals,
while all around other carers
answered phones and were busy.

The Cruel Prayer

What's that dear? Can't hear you.
Get me my coat. No. I'm going out.
Yes. That's right. That's right. Yes.
No. I'm going out today. Going out.
What's that dear? Can't hear you.
No, he hasn't come today.
My hat. Get me my hat. What's that?
Can't hear you dear. I'm cold.
Get me my hat dear. I'm so cold.'
As she lies bared on a bed,
talking to her daughter,
talking to the ceiling.

Or chants, 'Our Father /
Which art / in Heaven'
Over and over. Over and over.
Over and over.
Is this prayer?
Or sound roped by a rhythm,
each syllable as desperate
as hand-over-hand
defence against a flood?

Then is silent.
Bewilderment too is beyond her
as she's hoisted in a sling
and wheeled along a corridor,
just as they do a drip-stand.
Her nightgown caught above her waist,
the strap creased up into her crotch
like a G-string.

Weaning, At Any Age

That moment. A car slides away,
turns the corner and disappears.
In it my son. And he is gone.

My daughter, who was here,
– what, a minute ago? –
is now, merged somewhere

among others on a bus,
as the doors with a soft exhalation
ease shut.

Or just that they cannot keep waving
and walking backward – they turn, must turn
and face another kind of day.

And there's the moment too
when those whom now I watch,
are standing, holding themselves,

just themselves, until a car is lost
in traffic. And finally giving in, turn
and return; past the scent of daphne,

the red gravel crunching underfoot,
accepting with the breath
it is this space

which makes each day new.
It is absence we share
– like an embrace.

Of a Marriage

(for George and Elaine)

Of eighty-nine years there are now hours.
What's left is the shuffle of a queue –
like a passenger committed to a flight
whose details his disease had arranged,
whose instructions his body follows,
obediently, like all first-time travellers,
to the letter.

He shifts, wakens, morphine-bleary,
tries his old bluster, then immediately drops
away, as if suddenly called to answer
a knock at the front door
at the far end of the house,
as people come and sit and having set
there, touch him or look, then leave.

He becomes agitated
– his legs scissor under the sheet,
as if he is elsewhere, caught in a rip.
The effort exhausts, he sinks.
The body methodically continues its dying
while he, in their marital bed,
is stranded, is far from home.
Words disintegrate like leis
bobbing, separating and singular,
on a wide ocean.

His wife of sixty-two years
puts her lips to the waxed flesh of his face,
'Don't worry, dear. It's me.
It's only me.'

Finding Breath

(for Wendy, Brab and the girls)

Gael has found the Christmas card
in your handwriting, 'Wendy – Christmas 1989'
– and still we catch our breath.
Even the flat words of the news clipping
make us catch our breath.

A Sunday morning and we are still in bed
when the phone irritates. Your voice –
up, I daresay, for a breezy yarn,
'Russ, it's Brab… Wendy's dead.
I tried, Russ, I tried.'

What? From the mash of shock, tears,
words misshapen so they're only sound,
a name. A fact.
Not you though, Wendy. Not you.
But we are at a graveside
and all that district is there.

Your daughters skipping in new dresses,
shy at being dressed by so many
with their unusual gifts: of big men silent before them,
the faces of their wives tight as masks.
And their father who takes them over
to the edge to show them where Mummy is.

'I'm going to feed Danielle…
Brab, I can't breathe. I need my puffer.'
Your cry like a swimmer drowning.
Only it is you, young mother, our Wendy.
'Brab. Better get me to town.'
At the first gate you are unconscious.

'I keep hearing her calling, 'Quick,
Brab, quick.' I couldn't do a thing.
All day. Just rode the horse.
Couldn't see. I couldn't help crying.
For what the girls had lost.
That she wouldn't see them growing up.'

Our baby son cries in his sleep.
His mother gets up and goes to him.
And holds him. Holds him till he settles
into the even breathing of his little body.

And twenty-three years have taken air
before these words could find the breath
which that autumn evening you could not.

For Two Now Captive of That Moment

(Easter, 2011)

Yesterday, Sunday, a lazy day for an easy drive
out over the smoke-blue haze of a tablelands autumn
until a flash of headlights broke the spell to tell us
an accident so bad, up ahead, we'd better find another way.

Working the gravel of another route, among
the poplar-golds, their plumes in spilling cascades,
a quiet, sober riot of praise, the hessian-brown
of last season's grasses, the noiseless sheep,

how could one not think of what now was fact
on that other road? The miscalculation, the bewildering instant,
then the unalterable invasion. That somewhere
there, just like that, a sky had shattered and rained

tears of glass. There, among the glitter, life was undressing,
slipping from a life. Already, minutes had thickened,
one on one, like the drift of a poplar's falling leaves.

Already a fact was growing older and harder
among the parts of a cooling machine
and spilt fuel spiked and sickened the immediate air.

Driving back today I dread finding where
it occurred: was it at the long, sweeping bend
where the brown falcon sits and surveys,
or the tight corner at the bridge? Or up the hill,

that bit the Council needs to mend? Was that it, there?
Or there? That loose gravel splayed like a fan?
Nowhere the black testament of rubber, no parts untidy as
    litter.
Not a thing.

The brown falcon lifts from its post,
lifts up, then is lost somewhere
in the chilled blue. The valley
clamped in silence, holds itself, and aches.

Soon after, a driver in a ute,
his dogs lapping the wind,
he raises an open palm
from the wheel

as he passes, heading down that way.

After your service, Wal

I am driving back from the plainness of a church,
back down the way we came this morning for your funeral,
back through and back into the world,

back from where we had been collected into ourselves,
hearing the dumb hooves of words,
held by a damp, mizzling light there,

stripped and reduced and freed.
Each one of us – sharing like communion bread,
what we share with you – a death.

I am driving back through the light of an ordinary day
as if on a flight, descending into the torn waste of it.
It seems scrappy, dirty – the blown plastic wrapping,

the wearied brick shopfronts, its pouting adverts.
Do we have to come back to this?
The greasiness of it, a film on my skin.

The dead, we feel, are finer in their names,
even as already, as always, they've begun their erosion
in the memory.

Driving back I try to fix what I hadn't needed do before –
the more I try the less I grasp – your crooked smile,
the dry-leaf whisper of your voice, the skin cancers you earned

in Occupied Japan along with a heart lost to envy or bitterness –
they slip like steam venting from a factory.
I try, like looking at a star, to view you obliquely

but it hazes. This has happened before
yet learn again what it is we lose:
that there will be a name, a date, back there,

as when cleaning a desk we find an old Christmas card
and try hard to remember, knowing we've forgotten
what we want to capture.

In the early evening's dusty pink I see out into a paddock
two men returning to their vehicle bearing
a post between them. Steadily.

As if they are used to the weight and to each other,
And dropping it, they straighten.
One calls his dog. The work'll be there tomorrow.

Seeing them is a relief from all of this day.
Like your evening whisky, Wal, it's clear and steadying.
A day, its work, has ended, as it should.

A Scene on a Birthday Present's Wrapping Paper My Father Gave to Me

(i.m. Rod Edwards)

Certainly an English sky – pale blue, the mauve of rain,
and grey ballast for each blossomy cloud, and a pair
complete with horse brasses, feathered fetlocks;
a ploughman, cap and green weskit; a furrow turned,
the rest of the day untouched. The yeomanry of it!

This, a scene of farming I've never known, all Vaughan Williams,
it seemed my father's acceptance for the way I'd taken
which I knew I would ever since as a kid I smelt the apple-sweet breath
of a horse, the malt of cow shit and that bowed Devon man took me in:
with yarns and decency, his mild oaths and country Anglicanism,
his high croaking English voice, the absence of 'side', his contempt
– 'They're not farmers – they don't keep fowls',
his ploughman's trophies beside the whisky decanter.

He took me into the world of the little Fergy and the house
    cow;
the separator whose bell rang with each turn of the handle,
'Not too fast, or we'll both be in trouble';
setting fire in the gullies to bracken fern –
no matter the time of year. Standing there, his humped back
hooked over a shovel, his eyes red-rimmed, pale blue, watery,
drooping almost from their sockets, a drip at the end of his
    beaked nose
he'd wipe away with the back of his thumb. Skinny as
    Catweazle,
his mottled, weathered skin like lichen crusted on the rails of
    the yards.
A countryman.
A world of smell: dogs, harness, steaming cattle
sweated into your clothes, clover's sweet-sour fullness
in the streaming blue milk; of the muffled snuffle and chomp
of mouths working among the hacked swedes – those bruise-
    purple skins,
the dental-white flesh turning brown on the red basalt earth,
lumped like yellow turds the morning after snow.
The sump-gutting track, the massed rippling, like schools of
    fish breaching,
of ryegrass, all silver, in the late afternoon, late winter sun.

And death too: the cow in calving, and the calf;
the crow at an eye like a sharp reminder,
the sheepskin on the fence fresh after slaughter
like a parchment map with its pencil-red tracks
while the dogs slinked back and licked the stones clean.
Here, the sky over Werai was as soft-blue
and tumbling as anywhere in England.
And a boy was in love as much as ever he would be –
with a farm that already was on its way to becoming an island
– an old man, bucket in hand, bent, feeding his fowls,
a cloud that was blowing away.

Bloodlines, Stud Breeding

He is ageless, has always been.
He is Chinese. He is Harry.
And now he is in a room with a crucifix,
and photographs of children on ponies jumping,
or in new school uniforms, taken ten,
fifteen years ago. They'd be adults now,
with children of their own. Not his blood
but they are the only blood he has.
And a photo of him as a young man.
Impossible, it must be someone else.

There was only one man for this name.
A name from the simple generation
that knew nothing but work.
There was no past. He was just there.
He had come with the property
when the place changed hands
And they kept him on.

His hands thickened into paws from milking.
He jog-trotted, was ever deferential, stammered,
was hardly ever off the place, except for church,
though cattlemen spoke to him first.

He was not of their blood
and so, he is here in this room.
Anyone else would be adrift.
The staff like him: are very fond.
He does the gardens; is loved
in that useless way old age is.

Never married. Was there ever a girl?
One he fancied but being Chinese…

He was not of their blood
and so he is in a room,
that's quiet as a crucifix,
ponies forever lunging mid-flight,
the afternoon slumbering between meals.

Mr Markiel

Always, 'Shush, you kids!
Around the back!' or 'Please, Mrs Erwin,
the children, no noise. He try to sleep.'

We'd see him coming home from his second job
and remained concealed as he passed,
as one would, frozen by a feared animal.

Occasionally the smell of tobacco or a movement
their side of the palings, rustling as if threatening
to break through.

My mother said he'd been in the Polish Resistance,
and knew how to use piano wire. I was glad
he worked so much.

And that day I saw him at their clothes line,
his hands sticky with feathers and chicken blood.
Suddenly aware, he looked directly at me and grinned.

Mr Dunwoody's Voice

My father hands me it: 'You'd be interested in this,'
as if redirecting mail sent to the wrong address.
Two poems, handwritten, about love. Their words,
those of one used to working with other tools, not these;
by one shaping, as if from stone, a testament.

He surfaces out of memory much as he would
when, out for a Sunday drive, my father would stop
before a house walled by a thick laurel hedge
and disappear, leaving us, in the Austin A90, bickering,
our skins sticking to the seat. Our heads brassy
with the ran-tan of cicadas in the brick field heat
of that raw fibro suburb.

Then he would be there, filling the window
like some inquisitive animal in a game park,
awkwardly proffering his paw to my mother,
'Hello, Lorrna,' in that accent,
growlingly musical and lugubrious,
distant and troubling, like the sound, late at night,
of a train as it thundered south and then, was lost.

This, the accent heard in the house of my father's boyhood:
that house – its unforgiving Arctic bedrooms,
the improbably high ceilings, the unlit marble fireplaces:
house of the Presbyterian God.

The accent of lives I knew only as names
attached to photographs of thick-pelted men,
porcelain-delicate women – both unsentimental,
hard-eyed, for whom emotion unguarded
would always betray. A family of names,
stones in a wall, shelved as in a columbarium.

The letter ends, 'Dear Bob,
This is all
I have to show for a wasted life.'
What? What would bring someone to this?

The unforgiving rock of their faith,
its fearful judgment, or, in a loose moment,
like a maudlin drunk, he'd given into self-indulgence?
Both, I see now, as sides of the same coin –
this, his people's, my family's, maybe Ulster's, besetting flaw.

But what did he want from these poems,
their work-boot rhythms, the fettling clang of each rhyme?
The hours he gave to the stones of words, why?
Why pass them to my unpoetic father?

That he was son of people from Dromore and Bally-na-hinch,
all dead? And there was no other?
I can't tell. At too great a distance now,
these sheets of paper, thin as old skin, sing
to themselves, like family secrets.

I hear a heart bullied by Calvin's curse, still needing to sing.
This widower in his kitchen with its kerosene heater,
its teapot, its window like a cold eye, stumbling over verses,
addressing them to one who would not hear.

Their green and soft County Down, lost County Down,
and once again, they tumbling
in the rounded, grieving vowels. He singing to her
in the rumbling, uncut stones of that accent.

But most I hear those words which trouble –
'– a wasted life' – unalterable as inheritance,
implacable as an accusing finger.
Final as ashes.

Around the District

1.

Must be a good year:
he's shouted himself
a new set of teeth.

2. Saffron Thistles

Every year chest-high,
guarding the place –
a new idea hasn't intruded
there for years.

3. Spring blossom

Late snow snagged
on apple boughs

4. The Widower

Dark under dark pines
the house there somewhere.
Not even a TV's bloodless flicker.
He's in bed already.

5. Rainfall Records

How it varies – from one corner
of a paddock to another,
from one liar to another.

6. Road names

Older families never
use them, saying,
'Out our way.'

7.

No clocks here.
Only work
and its two hands.

8. Sharp, Sudden, Clean

Sunday afternoon
like a head muzzy with wine
until in the north-west
from where no thunder comes
a solid pounding
– someone giving the roos a touch-up

Not unusual
Still, we note it.

9. Standing Around

Boys grin like moons
when it's said
how they're taller
than their fathers,
stronger too, while
the men look at their hands,
rubbing them as if polishing a tool,
thinking what's to be done.

10. Keeping Faith

He throws a generic wave
but continues mowing
around the family graves.
Who will mow them next year?

11. A Nursery Wish

(for Isabelle)

In their trays I have lifted forests.
Now I want limbs to climb
in branches grown
from what I have sown.

Bigga

A house in a paddock
at the time of the midday meal
A curtain shivers
An axe rests in a stump
From under a cypress a dog, watchful, shifts,
Some links of its chain clip
each other
Under the pressure of clouds
a day balancing
Balanced
Just

Back Country

After miles of dirt roads
and the promises of maps
you stop and get out
as if unfolding wetly from a casing.

A cold day buffets the car,
the wind squeaks like the dry rub
of a finger along the duco. The radio
thin as a child fretting.

At the front gate, the flower beds,
so neat, like a hospital garden
but small, mean, you think,
in so huge a paddock.

The skin of a sheep, freshly slaughtered,
is slung along the side, its edges
beginning to curl. The head stares
from the grass. Silence is a pressure.

You find yourself rehearsing words
and your words seem foreign.
You realise how gauche they would sound.
A cloud slides over the cold mirror of a dam.

Peep in at a window – things in their order
– a kitchen, a table, a knife.
With nothing to check them
images spread like oil spilled.

The fantastic, the bizarre
are tropical flowers you have brought.
They wilt. You seem so silly.
Your car radio bleats, calling you.

You relatch the gate-chain and return.
Then as you scatter gravel the sense,
did something shift at a curtain?
Minutes later, you recognise the turn-off.

The world reorients itself.
The road back slides
like a trickle of whisky,
miles ease under, hills laze
in their slow ocean swell.

This is now landscape. You notice light
tipping things. The late sun warms.
Still, there's a window,
glazed cold with that glass-hard sky,
and a curtain, with a shivering edge.

And things in their order.

Meeting the school bus

A ute is parked in between trees,
the track is rubbed like skin over bone,
two fine lines scored in a paddock
through which she has come.
The wind pounds, the chassis rocks,
the radio may as well not be on.

Light slivers like glass splintering
from a chandelier, snow gums flow
in dull solder between the granite,
hard leaves clatter
as bunting in a used-car yard.

From the bus two cowled shapes,
puffballs of dust exploding at their feet.
Their voices, wind-garbled, broken
like the accents of travellers returning,
bringing words from a talking world.

On a Day of Power-line Maintenance

Notified duly – of course, as was their duty.
No excuses – I'd forgotten, of course.
So, this morning: … Off.
The radio mid-word,
the fridge slurred and shuddered.

There were trees blowing about outside,
magpies among the split and bowing crowns,
crows farther off. And farther off.

As if air off snow had chilled all about
this house was fresh, scoured.
Now I could hear its little noises,
murmurings, an only child talking to itself,

and thought how like those of the body
when the hours are a country hard under moonlight,
and we like a small animal in hiding, listen.
We, strangers, listening to the syllables of another tongue.

Shifting Silage under a Summer Moon

This tractor is an island, a speck, spilling light in a skirt about it:
beneath the footplate it falls like flour from a sieve and sows into the stubble.
A yolk, a bolus almost, it's solid in the cup my headlights cut from the dark.
Sitting here is like watching an animal shoving about with its nose.
Out at the farthest reach of illumination it weakens to a mist,
so that what's out there, the grey paddock, is furred with a nap,
tawny-sable like that of a Burmese cat.

Boulders of feed rear out of the dark,
like a coast suddenly realised before you,
their slumped bulk that of a mythic warrior brooding after defeat,
even as under moonlight the plastic wrap glistens wetly,
moulded and nubile – but iridescent-hard too like the bodies of beetles.
Dumped only this morning already they're ruined-proud
as those abandoned busts staring across a waste land
that was once a fabulous Durbar.

It's the thickness – the fermenting, molasses-sluggish, liquorice-heady smell
of grass melting in its sugars, the vat-full, brewery-maltiness of it,
along with the boorish persistence of diesel (its stink immediate
and insulting, that same efficiency as chloroform soaking a mask),
which gluts the night air like blood thickening in a drain.

The tractor rages only so far as its headlights. And bullocks
   into its work.
This little kingdom is as much as you command.
The night brings you everything else, as though it were an
   unfailing host
to a guest come suddenly among its tents.

You learn a new geography. The paddock you swore you
   could work blindfold
has shifted… And you're easily lost. Against the glitter-dust
   of stars
what you've known as landmarks gesture and menace like
   silhouettes
in a shadow play of another culture. Everywhere shadows of
   trees, rocks,
like oil stains on a tablecloth, watermark the moon-white
   earth.
Out of a felted dark that is close as sleep, a flash, a stare –
   cold, opalescent green
or red flaring. A blink, duck, bob, slink, lope, a scurry. And
   jinking: nothing.

And learn how another climate works: the air flowing like
   creeks;
the mother-comfort, cosy wrap of it, then a baptismal plunge
into a musk of mould and humus which pools in bog-cold
   pockets;
in the released scent of things, the rust-cumin and pepper-
   spice of earth,
the disinfectant eucalypt: the sloping of country from one
   smell to the next.

Earlier there were birds, their cries weaving nests above where
    they were to roost,
squabbling like voices from crowded tenements. Now, hear
    crickets,
their scritch a run of fine cracks; the earth give and creak,
readjusting, like a chair settled into.
And be taught how the moon in its passage forms from the
    night a day
that's as supple as well-oiled leather, comfortable, flexed, easy
    in its clothes.

It is true: it is coldest before dawn, before the tearing of
    darkness into scraps –
the reappearance of clouds filling with substance – even the
    racy cirrus ones,
combed-wet, now drying, streaming thinly as the hair of girls
    escaping on a Harley.
This paling into light, its anaemic pink and yellow, has the
    melancholy
you recall, of leaving a childhood bedroom before returning
    to school.

Approaching the house, its small hunched darkness like a
    stone,
is to feel the weight of a stone. Self-absorbed, it is alien in the
    new light.
Closer, it smells heavy with complication. And you, like a
    traveller returning,
accept that that other country, well, it was another country,

though getting down at the gate you breathe what lifts from
   the mown paddock
and wish, as you did as a child, you could live out under a sky
as fragrant as the idea of India, among the brilliance of stars,
on your island of light
and not have to stop.

Like the Word 'Artesian'

(for Les Murray)

'But came the long train of camels blowing drowsily:
Words paced, nodding, tinkled through my spirit'
                                              'Poet' – Francis Webb

My kids blaze like saints, their faces buffed by the wind,
'Dad! Dad! Come, look in the TSR! Camels!'
There, shaggy as rugs dumped, among pack-saddles
and paraphernalia, four mounds ruminate, have taken
    possession,
are immutable like Uluru or the Sphinx.

The children have never had the world surprise them
quite like this before. They stand at the fence and look.
This distance is close enough to the fabulous.

One lurches up as if there were a heaving of the earth.
Then the others. Their heads lifted like watchtowers,
out of which eyes pan, disinterested as a camera,
until a slow closing of an eyelid is the measure of contempt,

an imperiousness cultured from a history with us:
the cost of temples, the talcum dust ground from the bricks
    of empires,
a holy book's worn and fluttering pages.
Spices, opium, perfumes on the wind, the women taken and
    traded,
how life is blood cupped from a slit vein and mixed with the
    calf's milk.

From the fringes…the desert wadi, or staked by the nose
outside a city wall, witness to that queerly tottering creature
whose voice is weak immediately beyond the circle of fire-lit
    faces.
That voice, light and beguiling, yet like the wind, a knife.
Cruel, weak. Though always its hunger, its dependence.

It's in that neck, in the cynic's flex of it,
that suggests a thousand mile weariness;
and the lip lifted, snarling, the bitter acceptance.
The knobbed arthritic joints, a shambling of bones
as if it all were held only by their leather –

the sense these bodies were impossible machinery
threatening to break down but by grit or perverseness would
    never,
as beneath their load of sleepers a railway begins its length
and one Afghan, hard as silence and utterly lonely, at their head.
Next morning the TSR's empty. Flattened grass,
ashes, the wind. I see them elsewhere.
Occasionally, spores of dust puff into a white Tablelands sky,
as padding distance, they discard miles,
like the spirit which strips unbidden, needing nothing
but the light into which it heads.

They head out to the earth's curve. They and their freight,
an Australia now dated as telegraph, bull-wire, quart-pot,
a day's stage and a feed, rations, sandy blight, Johnny cakes,
even Jessie the elephant, the hide of, SP, 'cobber' or the Line
   of Lode,
re-entering, as water into sand, the silence of that artesian heart.

(TSR: a travelling stock reserve; Crown land set aside for stock
when being driven along the 'Long Paddock', this too becoming
obsolescent.)

The Budawangs

All that day scored by the undergrowth
which was as much within ourselves
as the whipping and sly entanglements,
and a cavernous bush occluding any sky,
we followed a map of little sound,
of trickling water, until dark
and slept when all seemed to slip
from us.
Then in the morning,
like a nest among thorns,
three feet away,
a pool of still water,
self-contained, like wisdom,
calmly held our faces
as we drank.

In Praise of *Forest Trees of Australia* – Hall, Johnston & Chippendale, Canberra 1970

Casuarina cunninghamiana – River She-Oak

It must be midday: gathered to it like flood-wrack is the dark.
The thatching of the cassowary's feathers has mothered shade
beneath its skirts. You know it will be cold there:
it will be matted with needles the colour of an Isa Brown hen,
white-flecked with fungi, must-thick in decay.
Beyond, light is pottery hard.

In their height, their shabbiness too, there is assurance, acceptance
– maybe from all they have withstood, have learned –
but as if a building had been exposed before completion
there is a construction site's confusion – of wire, matted
and complicated, thick as the tangle of a Pre-Raphaelite girl's hair,
the stiff necessity of cables, ugly, messy, blackened as if from work.
That chaos which needs demand and we ignore,
preferring beauty in the achieved form.

Self-sufficient, there is an air of indifference about them
like members of the upper class casually associating with their own.
The eye's interest drifts: off to the right a dense hedge of black,
a younger generation milling as young things do
and this you know means the glitter of water.
Out of these white-dry hills it is the music of this place,
a relief and balance, reassurance and laughter.

This fringe of deeply green seems like a refuge
for little noises: scurryings, scratchings, chips of song,
in the presence of all that steep concentration of silence,
solid in the summer heat. And so, this valley is preserved
from the knowledge of any other place. Apart, that is,
from summer's catalyst – smoke's first pale whisper.

Being noon, it is permanent as Luxor.
Then, a shift of air and the needles, delicate,
fine enough to be Asian, release a sigh
as clear, as defined, as you remember
of the coolness of water after exertion.
We think it speaks of our sorrows, our grief
but it is simply acceptance, like that, say, of a widow
left minding the farm. Each day measured.
The air passing through, like the breath.

It is still. It is midday. It alters.
Subtly, the sun carves new shields, pins new maps
onto trunks. Patterns appear, disappear like tidal islands.
And shade adjusts, resettling the flounce of its skirt.
A breeze lifts. The river escapes.
Like us, it cannot endure the soughing,
that even in summer, seems like the muted suffering of
   Neapolitan women.

Eucalyptus melliodora – Yellow Box

(i.m. Rob Murray who I heard today had died in a tractor accident)

There are the facts of botany, then there is the tree.
It is the tree of all that is solid and enduring:
those grandfathers left conferring in wheat paddocks.
The elders dotting the parks, silent and aboriginal and watchful.
It is torture to split, it hazes with bees, sweetens the air thick
with the small fizzing stars of its flowers. Like most box
it has fenced itself in, has burnt itself out in generations
of Rayburns, making scones for its honey.
From a distance it smokes a grey veil all over itself
like one an orchardist uses to camouflage his fruit
and everywhere it stands out like a natural leader among
ill-disciplined recruits; its shade black as corridors,
where stock fold and breathe softly through the heat.
It bends and grows through cracks in the air to be most
    eccentric;
great boughs like arms extending into hives or working
    through tunnels
or as if searching after the legs of a calf in the intricacies of
    labour.
It is the decent man, the honesty and plain-speaking and the
    class of it.

And this one we found on your place, Rob, all blue, strangely
    blue,
the blue of sepia photograph blue as if the sky were the weak
    wash of it,
it the original pot of colour. Its fruits clustered everywhere
almost glossy, shoe-polish-brown, apple-red. We swarmed
over its branches thinking this a treasure we might not see
to collect again as though it were an ancient city which would
easily disappear into the sands if we left off picking for that day.
That one day, Rob, we collected seed of that tree
and have not returned. Nothing can be returned.
Melliodora. Sweet honey hived in the memory, the tree endures.

Macquarie Pass

(for Lyn Miller)

This is the day of a picnic, first outing in a new car
and I am not yet stale with travelling –
flicker, glare, flicker.
The forest is chattering, loud to itself
– scurryings of song, flashes with leaves shivering,
the way things tell of suddenness, of absence
– as when a door has been closed, a curtain,
flowers in a vase, the air – all unsettled, uncertain.
And that primeval scent, that deep musk
that tells the world has mysteries which are always
here and this is something you will not forget.

Overhead, farther than the world of adults
talking their words in strange ways, almost
at the edge of that hazy blue, the dreaming future,
stretched tips of new growth, like the last of a coastline
disappearing into ozone. They're like fingerlings
in darting shoals, careless as a girlish wave;
as copper-bronzed as tanned skin they're teasing
the wind. All this abandon, and I am envious.

Flicker, glare, flicker, as strobed and dozing
we are cradled down, around, through.
Windows reflect our faces, our eyes stare
into the rush, silly with it, but wanting too
to seize just one moment in all that it is,
the impossible unchanging forever instant.
Fronds of fern droop like a dancer taking her final bow,
drops of water shaken by our mudguard, splash.
If they were sound, they would break silence with
the purity of bells.

Just here is moistness, the air as damp as the night-sky
is saturated in its dark. Wetness seeps, silver-bright
in the creases of the tannin-steeped sandstone,
freely as the unself-conscious singing of children
heard down in a street below.
Then, all around there is the presence of palisades.
They could be shafts of sunlight but the sun intervenes
and makes a temple of these columns.
Rose and Flooded Gum and shaggy Turpentine
mock Karnak, sing with a light Salisbury reaches after,
but there is no Old Testament here. Light is everywhere:
this world is leaved and awash in its spangle and glitter,
we shower in a confetti, our heads light in its froth.
Slowing for a corner, like hearing a party nearby,
there is ease, mingling and the silver sprinkling of sound.

Then out onto a ridge, a clearing where the sun has a chance,
out of the dark, down and around a switchback
and plunge deep again.
Today, though, there is no darkness:
this boy's heart lives into what he already knows,
what sacred means. This is not a day for lessons.
Just a day, as clear and bright and blue, as promising
as the beach to which we are heading.
All this among the one stillness of that almost tumbling,
austere ruin of the escarpment.
We brake at another corner and turn again.
Flicker, glare, flicker. Rejoice.

Eucalyptus saligna – Sydney Blue Gum

Descend, descend and the forest increases over you:
The biomass of shade, the change of rooms until light,
where allowed, is a tinkling of chandeliers.
A community hall of quiet elders watch as you pass
or that sense of just one whose gaze follows
with mild interest, as he might the changing weather.
Dropping, you skid over the white scree of a track,
the heat brilliant, a scattering of so many little suns,
and slip, your feet spearing the thatched roof of litter
through to the moistness of decay.
And overhead, everywhere,
small bunches of heads, opening, closing,
wind-silly and as ignorant of you as kids free of school.
Sometimes, animals, that shiver of disappearance,
sometimes birds, their cries like cries, urgent, and lost.
Mostly though it is air which visits here, packed with heat,
thick with smell the way a perfume is persistent
throughout a department store. But it pinches as from spices.
That said, this is not Bali – there is no indulgence in its
    cinnamon,
in the blue haze of its oil little forgiveness.

It has weight like stacked bales and will not shift,
until like a workman who has knocked off for the day
it changes clothes and swims with the late afternoon breezes
lazing in from the coast, frivolous with an excess of blue
and gauzy with moisture and salt. Ah! Those few hours of
    release
before night, sudden as a guillotine, refrigerates all this into
    stiff leather.
Otherwise this is a gated community, restrained as Quakers,
indifferent as all cities. You are not excluded but neither
is there welcome.
Yet standing here is to be surprised
by gifts of light spattered between the confusion
which is the massed stems of words, one masking another,
as deeper and deeper the eye searches, hungering for an end,
such as the certainty of a city upon a skyline
or a farm, calm and breathing easily into the dusk,
or simply for that clearing where there is no language.

Here then is your mind and your loneliness
as a branch breaks or limbs squeak, one rubbing
against another, and always the drift of things dropping
– the snakeskin of bark sloughed off, summer's ochre-burnt
    peelings,
small boats of leaves lost while unshaven old men ache and
    lean
uncertain they might ever recover from gravity.

And from a ridge you look across hills, crumbled black-green,
intensely self-absorbed, lumped like ploughed ground,
the massed crowns swaying like bull kelp in their dark oceans.
It will be a long climb out. You might not make it.
Held here, you might also come alive in its dream.

As Flames Were My Only Witness

After three days of wind pounding the midriff of hills
and nights of dry lightning fracturing the sky
into the crazing of old porcelain it was no surprise
when it came. In five minutes a towering cauliflower

was spilling white curds, froth and tumultuous blossom
a fractal coolly replicating from a moment
that was now far below, with birds
like flakes of soot tossed in its turbulence,
their cries plangent and scattering, and consumed.

Driving beneath into that apricot-soft light
was like being inside an evangelist's blimp:
a dome of chapel stillness, except for little flames
at the hem like small faces sneaking entry under.

For a moment there was a benign peace
as is said of those hazy, uncertain states:
the womb, anaesthesia, drowning.

We think we know silence, it is our blue Pacific:
the refrigerated, drained, arrhythmical kind,
and the cupped, hill-to-hill kind, with a dog's bark
or the crack of a breaking branch to give it scale.

This was something else – dense and pressing,
even in that beguiling peace,
vast and lonely as the space that clears
the moment before judgement.

Fire at Night

(for Phillip Price)

Tonight, the hills are ablaze. Everywhere, nests of coals,
cubed and collapsing, cosy and self-absorbed as slums,
sprawling as leisurely as an octopus. From stumps

blue gases squirt and flare, along fallen trunks flame
ripples like a flowing hem, tripping easily, confident
as a high-wire artist. Above us, the blown-out tents

and Medusa hair of it among the standing timber
erupting and tearing up the dark. You think of the sun
belching, coiling, far out into the cosmos.

It is as unworldly as a sleepy child's night ride
through industrial suburbs floodlit in orange.
Where you are is a fiction. Geography, approximate:
'Along that ridge. Up there. You'll see it.'

This is not your country. These are the hills of those
who come into town down back lanes, who, if they do,
sign their names slowly, who see, who remember,
who sometimes speak and though smiling, never tell.

We listen like immigrants. What they know is bred
from generations of silence: the split granite and winds
   screaming
about a farmhouse shaded beneath the cold fury of its pines.

Overhead there is a pummelling, all other sound flattened –
ugly as a locust, a helicopter consumes air, voices, thought,
thumping us with a matter-of-fact insolence

and screaming, is gone. Its intrusion has stolen our speech.
We feel puny. For a moment the fire seems more human.
Though rearing there are dragons unslayable, and the wind is
    fear.

In the morning, acrid and sodden, with a waterish citrus light,
we'll learn the reality of hills shrunken, like the shoulders of
    old men,
the smouldering verticals, corrugated iron dangling

like a beast with a broken leg, the house lost,
a truck camouflaged in the evidence of its escape
and in a corner of a paddock we pass,
slumped against a strainer, sheep stacked like sandbags.

Now though, all over us, roaring, roaring,
not the lost-in-itself silly menace of a football crowd
but singular, industrial, a breath-disembowelling thunder,

the one element of the universe, a ravening hunger,
pitiless as the solar wind,
and on this ridge we wait.

Parish Map

(for Phill)

In the fire tanker, talking our way into a map
we might need later that night. Our road, paddocks,
which have names, and histories, imprinted with nights
like these; where days manured into grass,

grass mulched in the bellies of stock long-slaughtered,
and little colonies of families, rosettes of lichen,
have disappeared like frost melting, in that unceasing migration,
into stories, into 'Ah, the Ross place. You'd be Marie's then?'

Stories hinted at in files and wills, in something
the elder partner of the solicitor's faintly remembers,
'Dad knew something about that. Nasty.'
Safe in grievances, fenced by yarns. Never fully finished,

of both the dispossessed adrift and the wary victors,
propped by the unforgiving dead. Stone on stone
kept neat as days graze past in silence.

'That's where the Chinaman had a crop
till they took to him. Still, you can see him
in some of the folk around town. You
have to know what not to know.
There's more out through there
than old bottles and quince trees.'

He's let me in, just this bit and I know
I'll have to pay him back some time.
Like if there's something I know –
though he's heard all I ever will;

that stories are as much as the flowing weather
he cannot help but live in. He grins,
looks straight ahead as if he hadn't heard
or sounds surprised, to make me feel included.

These hills fenced and snug in a map
The Lands Office could never find.
But now it is all black. The sky is burning.
A story twists around itself like a leaf ignited

as fires slumbering in their coals
murmur underground.

D Ward

So: they're whoopee-free – like kids – to do what they please.
Though they keep looking at us as if we're new, from the big
  school.
It's clear, we're different: too big, too noisy, and stained with
  elsewhere;
our skin a little too coarse beside the fine linen of their faces,
but courteously, curiously they persist, fingering for a key
  which might connect.

They remind me of photos of men
banked against a grey stone wall in a bleak Ayrshire sun
recovering from Ypres. Sunken-cheeked, staring
as if through gauze. Pretty much the same as us
but wary though – not wanting to join in.

Some concentrate on the next step, each shuffle
stolen from impossibility like a mountaineer's
achieved at altitude. Some even seem at ease
– like lions stretched out behind a moat at an open-range zoo,
waiting the day's next big thing, food…maybe;

sprawling, hair, skin, genitals escaping confinement,
ample as a satisfied uncle after Christmas dinner.
There are even those who like royalty smile benignly,
blissful and gracious within their own, ever-sunny kingdom.

Here, bent over a cane, a frame, bodies contract
like a claw to the shape of a question mark.
The question hovers like a fluttering kestrel.
It's we who want an answer that might save us

from what we see, while they grip whatever's to hand
as if it were their only friend in a crowd of strangers
and gaze down to the far end of the corridor
– out to the limit of the known world.

The Big Picture

Outside, we know there is traffic, we have come from there.
In here they are immune. No weather either, only
the bathe and hum of a constant temperature, the
    unwavering fluorescent light.

Walking past each room is like peering into a display at an
    aquarium:
furniture placed the way rocks are used – that awkward,
    natural touch.
There's the feel of a warehouse, shadows with the drapery of
    drop– sheets.

Mostly you notice photographs, in ranks, by which the
    fortunate assert
they're not alone. And everywhere little clutter abets the lie,
bits and pieces, stuff – as if stemming a dyke. But it collapses:

the neglected meal, the zimmer frame in the corner
like a patient visitor. The birthday card from the staff.
Walking the corridor (thread to the world from which you've
    descended)

is like accompanying a slow version of Muybridge's images.
From each room, in a corner, a flat screen flickers with
the same daytime soap opera. Flick, flick, as you pass,

all that glossy youth, polished like apples, gorgeous breasts
filling this room, and the next. The volume's up high as if
    each's playing
to an empty cinema. Their audience dozes, gapes.

They've the substance of twisted sheets.
Their bodies like reefs exposed at low tide, they slip submarine,
beyond the comfort of the light in which we stand,

as if we are at the end of a jetty looking into the seductive
    depth,
and find ourselves speaking a little too loudly
as if calling for them to return.

The March

Pitt Street. Just after the Dawn Service, April '08, my first.
I'm here because somehow I want to have my father back,
to take him from the photos taken only three years ago,
– when he was pink-cheeked, sure-footed, erect –
and have him back.' Hey Bob! Hey Pa! Dad! Over here!'

I feel a fraud, small and unwashed, wearing his service medals,
The street's deserted, the crowd's ducked off
– the early-opening McDonalds is jostling-busy.
Workers from a Sydney City Council truck hose the gutters.
Their fluoro jackets, loudly yellow in the opening light,

that's grey and weak after the warmer dark, as it slides
across the upper windows further up the street,
fanning like the last of a wave over a hard sand.
Adapting, it softens. And we are given our daytime shapes.

Then a digger steps out, from the other side of the street and crosses,
not drunkenly but unsteadily. As if there were no other option.
Not on the arm of a son nor holding the hand of a grandchild.
Not even a mate keeping pace.

He heads east, steadies himself against the building on the corner
as a gust thumps into him like a boxer. He bends into the light,
to the coming day, to the next few hours, to what he remembers
of faces.

And I think of that newsreel of a young man capering down
   Martin Place
and how the crowds had seemed to part for him.

'…those beautiful young men'

(R.A.G. Holmes)

A soldier from the last war,
my father never spoke about it.
Neither did any other digger
I met at the Sydney March
after his death. They were still chiacking
'Blue' or 'Snow – that bloody fool'
Or 'Christ, he had an eye', yarns
how they nicked stuff from the Yanks,
right from under their noses.
Poor, silly, bastards. And
what a prick Blamey was.

Only you, RAG, allowed me into your war
– R.M.O. at Milne Bay and Shaggy Ridge,
you told me how, even now,
when the dark is close
as the wall of a dripping tent
the eyes of your friend haunt you,
who, coming to, realises how much his face
has been blown away
when standing by his cot you'd asked,
'Who, then, is this poor coot?'
In his eyes the plea.

Looking for your mob

I barely register they have passed.
They go past so quickly, so quickly,
Their banners have got them covered,
their campaigns – names held by two youths.
Most of the yarns – they've already gone to ground.

They go past, in the gnarled roots of their bodies,
in chairs, in defiance, down George Street
among flags, children, our untested faces,
and out of sight.

I look for your mob. But they've been folded
in with a couple of others. 'Folded'.
I want to see you as you appear in photos taken last year –
that eruption of a smile as you saw us.
I want to see you. But you're not here.

For a moment George Street is empty,
ahead the last bands deflate and a pause,
as if the crowd's not quite sure it's appropriate
to break across that space.

Then the traffic noses back
like water spilling into a dry creek.
Even the pubs seem just businesslike this year
– not rowdy with men remembering and forgetting.

The Coupling of Names and Places, 1941–

(One of my parents' generation speaks)

Strange when those names first came among us,
– those sounds' jangling, sing-song silly.
'Where?' 'How do you say it?'
Then, too soon, we learned to fill the belly
of them with a meaning our boys' absence gave.

And thereafter could not remember
when they hadn't been linked: a telegram,
an hour; a flat kind of silence in our street
married to a name we couldn't pronounce;

when farms hadn't buried themselves in work,
when the shadow grief hadn't hovered over us
and always, as if in the wind, the breath of syllables
we couldn't bear to hear but knew were fact.

In those years, uniform with loss,
which was a kind of weather,
faces slipped unnoticed, voices, too.
Girls in Accounts, who promised not to forget,

to keep in touch, heard mention of the shy boy,
and asking 'Who?' were hurt
because they could cry only a little.
Or a bit too much.

In those years names were all we had
which murmured among us
like bees working a sad garden.

Cousin Danny and Aitape, Ioribaiwa and Johnno
from over the way, and Bob, our Bobby,
shy-boy, smiling from the mulch and litter of Buna.
They flicker like leaves in a jungle light,

tangled in sounds, in those names
with which we have had to live,
that even now we cannot bring
ourselves to speak.

Ah! The stars of Rajasthan

(for Mary and Peter Zoller)

That night! With its voices we first met as a hum,
then increasing, like liquid simmering, insects gathering,
and light from the desert shrank,
the sun dying theatrically as we expect the sun to do,
while his people stamped rhythm into the dust, the dust into
    perfume; perfume, memory.

All night: the insistent feet, the clack of sticks and that
    drumbeat – milled like grain flowing,
as hazed, gauzed by dust, they turned and counter-turned
    and beat and beat and beat,
voicing what they knew of the earth beneath their feet,
each syllable a link hammered into a slinking, humming chain:
all of us held there in that dust and torch-lit circle.

Another night out in that desert: after the transvestite dancers
had been accepted back into the darkness an old man
    squeezes, wheezes from a harmonium
bronchial, attenuated, witching notes
and his family draws close to the coals, which settling, glow
    as if precious, and urge,

'No, Uncle, you must sing this. Please, we beg you.'
He does, hundreds of lines. Eyes closed, Urdu lifts, bearing
    every generation's song of love,
incongruous from such a voice, cracked and old-man-wavery
    and unshakeable,
lifts and tilts and falls, and is lost again,
the same way ash feathers upwards from a fire
or the way we try to retrieve a scent, faint from a childhood,
    now far-off.

And you become aware of a murmuring –
of all their voices as they bear this hymn beyond the firelight,
and in turn are carried by it,
out into a dark where the self is happy once again to be lost.

Even those who have come back from offices in Delhi, Montreal, Dubai,
in the delicate pastels of new wealth, cannot help these verses in little clouds of breath
slip from them like prayers, like promises,
out into the thorn-sharp of the desert. Coals spill, cool, blacken.

Sparks in a last shower swarm towards stars, which remote and hard, burn to diamonds.
All over us, the cold voice of ancestors singing the stern comfort of unbending verities.
And these songs, his voice, that wheel of bodies turning,
the unstoppable utterance of every generation flowering yet again
under the one sky of the indifferent ages.

This music, broken open with the heartbreak which sings in us all,
with joy, with grief, with India's gift, the acceptance of acceptance,
here, passionately, unaffectedly, reverently,
on these two nights in spring in Holi, in the desert with its thorn, under the stars of Rajasthan.

Amritsar

India is pitiless: it's a shock to realise
you are nothing: the barefoot women
bearing baskets of stones in the early slush
of Simla do not look up as we pass; the marigolds
bobbing on the Ganges at Haridwar, golden
and drowning, each a life and adrift;
the ghats, their dead lying in the sun;
the performing bear staked by its snoozing master,
raked thin as the sullen cows of Delhi.
You are nothing, as you pass
the idiocy of those inching their puja
face-down along the heat-softened tar.
You are nothing but a spoiled child
being taken out beyond your scented garden.

And yet: that morning, 6 a.m.,
around the streets of Amritsar –
the dust smoking like incense:
from carts, and trucks, and hooves,
already so many feet – I walked
into that haze and was consumed.

The Kathak Dancer: Mandawa, Holi, 2002

(for Lyn)

One night in a lifetime: the elephant gate of the castle,
rugs on the dust, monkeys leaping in, through, out the upper windows,
their arms like festoons, and now, the sun cooled, the walls breathing heat
as music opens like exploring fingers of water and so, surely enveloping,
eases us out of ourselves.
Then suddenly, drama flowering like clouds building into their tumult,
there beneath the light of flares – myths in huge shadows thrown up
against the palace walls. Their truths more vivid than any image
I saw as a child, lighting up the night-sky at the Chullora drive-in.

This from the body of the Kathak dancer: her hands piercing the dark,
entreating it, then teasingly retreating and so,
like the forming of love, the subtle unfolding of our lives
in a story: light sliding like snakes over her body
reminding us of how limited are the days of our vitality,
the delight in being – the mounds of her breasts given
to all of us and to her lover, the dark.

We so near this mystery burn with the life just beyond the
 flares.
Through her body the story, so intimate, of the gods and
 their loves,
the arrow and the deer, the chase, the certainty of pain,
the smugness of evil, the frailty of good, the phoenix of love.
And in its resolution, a drawing from us in the last release of
 our breaths
acknowledgement of what it is that lives there, what we have
 learned,
how we have been changed, – yes, exalted, humbled, seeing
 our companions
as if their faces had been washed, and we now seeing with our
 hearts.
All this given in the flowing movement, the fluid moment –
fulfilled in the giving and lost as soon as we receive.

Already she has disappeared to again become one of us
just as the dance has entered the dark, where it lives
and although not understanding, we realise
how we live in the same world as the gods. In a dance.

Lights Across Autumn Paddocks

Bottoming each dip my headlights plunge into a vat of milk.
Then surfacing, flung out beyond the gravel's spatter, is a
    starched linen.

Sometimes, on the horizon, chips of light, watchful eyes
before they turn back into the scrub. And then: nothing.

And the wind and the engine roaring.
Over farmhouse windows, buttery-fat or dull with a fish-eyed
    glaze

the moon squats, bloated and imperturbable and unsettling.
While those pale yellow squares at a distance are lonely as a
    train battling the dark.

Along the sides of a moonlit shed there's a frosted sheen,
with growth at their edges, lipped like coral.

Inside, a stuttering blue flashes up shadows of a man
as though a menacing giant in the retelling of a legend.

He is welding the small hours into something the farm needs,
straining days together the way he fences the unruly, pointless
    acres,

wearing silence like a work-hardened coat as he fashions a gift
he wants to place into the hands of his son.

The son, who wants a life, not a way of life, not a weight,
who wants things and is not here,

'Not here. Not here' drips at a pinhole weeping from the tank,
with cold pearls soldered around each rung, encrusted with
    its sad lustre.

The cold is as solid as the purlins and rafters as he stoops,
then rises, unbending, and steps around in the flare of his
   own illumination.
Two weeks ago all across the district light trailed behind tractors
like the train of a wedding gown. Everywhere, small satellites

were charting across the dark, blips on a monitor. Light fell
under tyres and combed like seed into the clods, the dark.

Next day: acres rigid as if sheeted under rusted corrugated iron,
stiff and salted with this, the first frost. Starched neat as
   1950s school uniform,

everywhere the crisping of furrows, the crust and glitter of
   broken glass
and later, thawing, across the valley a shimmering like the last
   notes of a violin.

And magpies carolling, fling choirs of sound, liquid and
   quarrelling, up and dissolving
across a white world, into the unstained blue, as if here, at
   last, were our golden home.

Now, though, to my right – the one light
that seems the most intimate – red towels of it tortured

and whipped by gusts of its own making. From a piled windrow
twisted flags and flung boulders of heat, which punch and
   gape and devour.

I want to stop and standing there, be folded into this —
the gift, like love, of heat but how could you explain yourself?

Smoke though, finds a way into the cabin. It catches me,
like yellow box honey — that immediate, harsh sweet fullness —

with that day we picked up sticks for a bonfire and I smelt
    blue smoke in your hair.
And I smelled it again and again as if it were something I knew

I would need to keep.

The road keeps falling under like a crop being headed.
The miles coil, uncoil, entangle in dust.

And each light, a pinprick in a sparse constellation, some
    puny as an anxious parent calling
into the unanswering dark, some burning cold in their
    disinterested, electric way,

courted by the blundering attention of moths, until a dog barks,
headlights flood the drive, and die. Then voices. Maybe.

Too late for fires to be lit, when I get there, my house, the
    stars swimming in its windows,
will show me to my bed and I will sleep in my clothes,

with smoke creased in them from that blaze back there,
those fires which surely must have died down by now.

Otters at Mogo Zoo

Some notes, some words, scraps which I find
and they appear – lithe, all slippery, alert and alive,
like an entertainer so popular he can get away with anything.

How effortlessly they please – 'Clap your hands. Clap,'
squeak their needle-sharp calls, and we do.
They're combed, slick-sleek, streetwise like vicious thugs –
dressed to kill,

eyes eying not us but the electricity, the flow,
the where? – where? scurry. And spotted,
the all-out brazen assault on the victim of their charm.

These pure athletes – all body, all go, all attent, already there
    at the next thing.
Even now writing this just the word of them swamps their
    enclosure
splashing life everywhere.

The notes of what I was going to say about you, us,
like the scraps a crowd leaves, being drawn on:
the otters, smarmy, confident, now laying siege to a new lot
    at the other end of the pool.

Hear it: the squeals, the giggles, the little, deep sigh of
    delight, 'ohh',
– not unlike that low moan the body gives up
being hurt.

Country Show Fantasy

I want to be on that horse, high there,
on that bay, whose neck arches
like the Sydney Harbour Bridge, and arrogant,
flexes like a Verrocchio, above the centuries.

I want a simple blue rosette fixed to the bridle
by the Miss Showgirl of that year, while
the one I ache for stands among the crowd
outside the ring, most womanly and calm
among her children, and catching sight,
gives a shy, girlish wave. I want her

to be looking up, shielding her face
as the mare stamps and chafes and skitters
and the crushed grass gives up its bruised sweetness,
and the sound of the PA echoes around the ground,
echoes out beyond the car park, the squeals of the amusement
    rides,
out over the dumb farms, and forever.

And I ride – wordlessly, insolently, into her heart,
into the days she has left
which we shall unthinkingly squander.

The Autumn Break

(Yes, Isabelle, you)

At my desk clouds are accumulating.
Out of silence, the spindrift and wisp
of the hesitant word, wavering.
Then: one or two, a spatter, little claws skittering,
a brief tattoo on corrugated iron,
clipped as the strike of a typewriter's keys,
A drummer counting in.

A pause. Then all excess – a spillage,
wanton as a racket of ball bearings
tumbling – loud as applause,
the first writing on a summer's earth,
and its perfume.

This rain of a new season,
the announcement of you.

The Red Enamel Bangle

This grey day in the full clamp of winter, bright berry,
red berry the eye picks out from a hawthorn's tangle.

Red breast, blazing breast, a crimson rosella
loud in the cold air, brilliant in its heraldry.

On the galvanised tray of the ute a bead of blood
– from a lamb, fresh – dropped today

until a crow picked life out through an eye.
Why mention this at all? I note a skin

hardening like enamel. Cooling, it clouds
but the blood's intense fire still burns.

And I return to a keepsake, a bangle you wore:
of carnations or poppies, their bright red bursting

beneath the cool-sheen surface – an eruption,
such as I felt seeing you in a crowded place,

or now, sharper, remembering, as I go
among ewes and crows in a lambing paddock.

Those flowers that cannot flower, they will not die.
So: this poem, bright with blood, a bloom of love,

keep it, will you, bury it in your heart
no matter how the days cool and harden?

And Still

If I were so blessed I'd say, 'Prayers
are the breaths of angels. Stones in the river
utter their faith and water, their rippling praise.
The tree offers its frailest twig for the wind
to bless. Listen to the wind. Take a stone
into your hand. Immerse yourself
in the singing waters.'

I am sorry; there are only the unending galaxies,
which came out of nothing. There is nothing.
There is utterance but there is no reply.
We don't endure suffering to stand
in a transcendent light the angels would burn for.
There is this earth, and the cosmos of one fact:
you are not here.

If words were lamps, were true, were anything
but the windy posturing of sound I'd believe
the theology of stones, the hymns of water,
the grace and sacrifice of the autumnal fall,
each proclaiming,'The one you love is not far.
She is here and all around. Accept this is
how love is.'

I am sorry. The stone is a fist, the smiling water
treacherous as a double agent; eaten from within
as by doubt, the tree is mute in its own grief.
The breath is all I know of prayer.
With my body I pray, and still,
you are not here.

Thinking of Student Accommodation, Glebe

(for Adelina)

Who moves in the next room?
Whose footsteps outside your door?
These walls a skin, a screen,
hear other lives *en passant*:

lovers in their urgency
press the cool plaster.
You cannot avoid the hunger
of their feeding. Caged,
awkward, you tiptoe about.

Or the homesick student, lost
as an abandoned calf,
slipping in, out, huddled in his shadow;
or that neat man from the country

they say has come to concentrate
on an illness and how he is to die.
Each breath, raw and jagged
and deliberate. Each numbered.

A shift of sound: the music of keys.
Then: clues, like tracks in the sand.
In the brush of cloth – haste? Or escape?
An impulsive kiss clinched in the tango

of a light and a heavier tread? Or,
is that pause the long intake,
the measured breath, that seems almost a decision
before a weight must be taken up again?

The door opens, closes.
Footsteps melt into the other world
of the street. Silence heals itself.
You pass the day procrastinating that essay.

Then, hearing footsteps return,
each as recognisable as a face,
you realise how subtly you've entered
the unspoken intimacies of another life.

They may have been fictions
but now, at this other end of a life,
accept how you were as close as ever
to knowing any other.

As you said, my dear,
'Not love, not even love is enough.'
There are lives in passing
and there is silence between.

www.ingramcontent.com/pod-product-compliance
Lightning Source LLC
Chambersburg PA
CBHW070920080526
44589CB00013B/1382